Dear Nora,

Dear Nova,

c. michael kinsella

QUERENCIA

Querencia Press
Chicago Illinois

ISBN 978 1 959118 61 9

www.querenciapress.com

First Published in 2023

Querencia Press, LLC
Chicago IL

Printed & Bound in the United States of America

AV,

    I have never seen anyone work as hard as you that wasn't putting nails in wood. Thank you for being consistently impressive, admirable, and exciting.

Dear Nora,

this ain't a love letter,
but i'm sure it'll come up,
cause darling i'm still hung up on you.

some days i wake up staring over at your side
of the sheets,
and in that brief moment before the pain sets
in,
i convince myself that you must be in the
shower;
you're walking the dog,
you're in the kitchen making pancakes,
and maybe you are, but it's not our shower.
it's not our dog.
they're not my pancakes;
they're his.

i carried you for years,
and when i couldn't, you disappeared;
taking with you what little fight i had—
but i'm not writing you to rehash how you
trashed
the few parts of me that were decent,
or to explain how i've managed to maintain all
the ways that i resent you—
i do though, if you could ever think i fucking
didn't.

i miss you, all of you, every fucking piece of
you.
the way you'd dance in the passenger seat of
that old truck,
the way you'd make me feel like i was enough

when i'd wake up to you already awake, looking
at me,
keeping me safe.

he misses you too i'm sure,
when you're living in my mind again.

this ain't a love letter,
but i'm still in love with you.

Dear Nora,

this ain't a love letter,
cause even though i held her in my hands,
we never really got a chance.

it's been years now,
and i'm still living in those same fears
from the day you told me—
my tears that same mix of joy and shame.
i was scared and ill-prepared like my own
parents—
i was selfishly concerned about the havoc
she'd play
on my own childish errands;
i refused to pick names—
wouldn't look at a single picture you framed.

    scared.
scared i'd be him.
    scared i'd fail her.
scared i'd succeed, and maybe even like it.

but you carried her, and i carried you,

and what was frightening became exciting,
and the excitement grew with her, with you;

excitement to pick names, excitement to play
games, to abstain and change lanes—
to be some sort of stand-up guy
like in all those springsteen songs that
aren't about cars,
and girls,
and sad proms.

but i'm not writing to daydream on what could
have been,
cause when the disappointments set in,
i took it upon myself to eat your sins—
while mine began to fester in the shadows
again.
and the relief i felt beneath my grief
has been enough to treat myself like a dying
man every day since—
instead of cherishing her memory i've been
using them to bury me;

and every day i am so fucking sorry.

this ain't a love letter,
but i promise i would've tried,
thank god no one let me.

Dear Nora,

this ain't a love letter,
and i'm not writing to forgive you—
though i'd love to hear you ask.

your memories have kept my misery
company since my early twenties,
they play friendly, but i know
when an enemy is tryna end me;
tryna put me back in the gutter
where i belong, but i putter on,
anything but strong, sanity gone.
call me wrong, but my salvation
is coming along—slow as it may seem—
even though i still dream that same
dream of you wrapped in a noose
of crisp white linens;
your milky skin pressed tight against
the wall and my calloused hands
chasing goosebumps across invisible
verses on your sweat-soaked body
all fucking night—

call them delusions,
call out my reclusion—
my thoughts are confusing,
but i wish you'd call at all.

in my mind it's always fall,
in my mind it's a forever brawl
between joy and suffering;
like a mansell score setting the tone
while you're being assaulted—
like unconditional love being force-bred

with gall and wormwood—

and there's always hot chocolate,
that's perfectly salted.

this ain't a love letter,
'cause i wouldn't even know
where to fucking send it.

Dear Nora,

this ain't a love letter,
but i chased everyone else away,
so i'm back to pretending you'll listen.

this hole in my elbow
where i use a needle as shovel
to bury all kinds of trouble
is starting to look like that dimple
on your inner thigh.

i'm too dehydrated to cry,
but i swear i'm not high.
it's natural to jump—
with wings made of dust—
yet expect to fly.

i swear i'm not high.

it's natural to think i'll never die
when suffering's immortal
and passed through generations.

i swear i'm not high.

i swear i'm not high.

listen, i swear i'm not high.

this ain't a love letter,
and it ain't a confession,
cause i swear i'm not high.

Dear Nora,

this ain't a love letter,
in fact you can go fuck yourself.
ya, maybe i'm a little bitter.

fuck you.
and fuck your hypocritical mom.
fuck your cousin, he's a little prick.
i wish he had died in that fucking crash,
this world could do without his entitled ass.

fuck your arrogant little brothers who think
they've seen trauma; they ain't know the taste
of a belt like i do.
and fuck you, and all your sheltered world
views.
in fact, fuck your whole world,
you know, the one i gave you with these
fucking aching hands.

fuck your memories, i hope i sour every last
one of 'em.
you best not have a single positive fucking
thought about me,
after leaving me like some back-alley
panhandler you tell you ain't got no change,
while the whole street can hear your purse
jingling on the way to a show, with tickets i
probably fucking paid for.
kinda like how i worked my ass off to pay
every fucking bill while you worked on
occasion to fill your own fucking bank
account.

fuck you, and fuck your fucking dreams,
you know, the ones we dreamt together?
the ones i built you while chained up in
leather?
the ones we swore we'd share forever?
these days i'm dreaming never.

fuck you and fuck your husband;
the guy probably doesn't own a single pair of
blue jeans.
fuck that clown. i'd like to grab him by his
hippy hair and stick him in the fucking
ground.
fuck you both for the happiness you found,
seeing as it's barely march
and this year i'm already at a fucking pound,
but at least it's got me feeling all profound.

congratulations on the daughter, i hope you're
proud.

i hope she grows up with some fucking morals,
but fuck me if i don't have my doubts.

this ain't a love letter,
like i said, fuck you,
but i'll probably want you back tomorrow.

Dear Nora,

this ain't a love letter,
but my male privilege is paying dividends,
and someone needs to reel me in.

i'm spinning in circles again,
i just can't find my bearings.
forever chasing a win,
i'm climbing a ladder that just goes round and
round,
it don't go up,
but it sure goes down.

i feel flimsy, when all these lies get me in,
and i might place, but the medals plated,
this whole schtick that i created
is nothing now that i'm deflated,
and i ain't been treated all that horribly,
but it was all horrible to me,
and if you'd just see what i call trauma
as my reality,
maybe i could swear to be everything you swore
to see
in me.
maybe i'd get up from this sore knee,
and stop begging for some divinity
to set me free from cages built on my belief.

this ain't a love letter
and if you think what i was is worth what i am—
well damn, you really were my chance.

Dear Nora,

this ain't a love letter,
it's just some more attention
for someone i'm pretending to hate.

it's hammering outside.

    the way it rattles the roof right
outside this window is reminiscent of when it
riddles the rivers i fish in; that being the
only time i don't feel like i'm in prison,
it's ironic that every time i hear it i'm
imprisoned in decisions that cost me you. or
maybe it was indecision, brought on by
perfectionism that stems from fearing i might
fail, even though all i am is failure—does
that mean i'm afraid of me? maybe i need a
saviour; maybe you could come back and save
your once beloved stranger?

    darling, it's like a cataclysm every
time i walk the catacombs of my mind and find
it setting in on you with that obsessive
precision, like i was gifted single-mindedness
and i'm counting tires on passing trucks
again. maybe i need an exorcism to exorcise
these scattered visions of our hands swinging
back and forth in unison. maybe i need an
acute incision to drastically dissect and
disassemble all the issues that remain for me
to address in regards to you and that white
dress? but for that i'd need a surgeon, and
there's a pretty clear division between myself
and someone in that position.

you see, they see us as animals, and
though there may be a cannibal within me, i'm
not one to feed in person; i'm not one to
shake hands and hold eye contact, unless it's
when i'm attacked by the man that looks just
like me—sounds just like me—living behind this
white-dusted mirror. so for now, i'll walk
those catacombs i mentioned earlier, despite
the weather getting eerier, and all the terror
i feel in here.

drizzle. drip. dribble

water breaches a crack in the ceiling-arch of
these crumbling halls.

	rapid rains run rabidly down my clothes,
and the devilishly determined drops that
tactically trickle through the torn, tattered
tears that tarnish this thrashed top, seem to
systematically shock sullied skin alive again,
almost.

	but it's only make-believe, like
children flying off garage roofs to land on
broken wheels. see, that's when they realize
that their arms aren't wings, and what was
once landing gear is now fractured, shattered
heels. that's when they realize that they are
not aero planes at all, only foolish little
boys.

	i carry scars from similar failed
attempts at aviation, and i've been maimed by
accomplishments, and i wear wounds from

pretending i've still got it; but i know the
truth. i know i'm a rusted-out version of what
i was in youth, i know i'm hollow without you.

    but the thing is, all that pain is never
going anywhere, cause i'm still dealing with
him and his mustached, monstrous grin. he who
planted sin inside of me before even puberty.
so wrapped up in the demon within. so wrapped
up in history, how could i ever expect to
deserve you, with the minimal effort i had for
anything outside my revenge...

    there's a draft in this room every time
i write to you. the dog doesn't seem to notice
it, even though i bathed him this afternoon—

you know, you've still got this power over me
that makes me cower when i'm flipping pages
and end up one too deep in albums i keep—
though by now should surely have disposed of—
despite how i despise how destroyed the
decrepit pictures might be, from years of
tears that i weep every time your face jumps
free of this carcinogenic collection i covet.
i scream. every single time, i scream, but my
voice can't escape the screen door of that old
apartment we ain't in anymore.

    it's still in almost every dream i
dream— at least one of four. we never shoulda
moved. i never shoulda left, but i had so much
to prove to everyone that knew me when, and i
had those false ideas of what they would
expect from me then.

who knew that bet could cause me to lose
everything i'd built since you filled my
emptiness? who knew that bet would cost me
nightly your sweet calming breaths on my
chest, each exhalation sweeping away the
frustration of my anxieties. each inhalation
taking captive my neurosis— so quickly you're
sweet slumbering safe-haven became necessity.
it's somber really, to think about what could
have been and what instead became.

    now my contempt is boiling over and
everyday i'm feeling older, these leather
shackles that bind me to my past, have bound
themselves to my flesh—and darling, leather
cracks.

this ain't a love letter, it's an apology, and
it's a goodbye, so i'm sorry, and i love you,
and goodbye.

Dear Nora,

this ain't a love letter,
it's the last letter—
just like that last letter.

these days i do what i can to hide my
vulnerability;
like all those days that i tried to live
honourably
were somehow just dishonouring me—
and i think that's why underneath
we both knew it wouldn't work.

the dog is walking into walls now,
but he still perks up when i call your name
aloud—
and my demons, they're all talking like hell's
about to break loose;

how?

maybe cause i'm still wearing that same noose
like a necktie;
loose—
i still can't tie 'em without you.

lately i've had this nagging need to
reproduce,
to create something that i could use
to crawl nostalgically through what skewed all
my views.
i could nurture them with all these tools
to avoid the abuse that had me designed to
lose.

but i think my demons had the same idea,
and without you i don't have a clue,
so i talk to this pen and pretend it's you—
so i can get all of this off my chest—

but it's not you, is it?
you're flesh and blood,
you're thoughts and ideas that conflict with
my own.
and i hate that.
i can control a page,
one of few situations where i actually win.
and goddamn it if i ain't sick of counting
losses with this knife on my skin.

so yea, i live my life like its roulette.
years have passed and i don't know what to do
yet,
so i scream at the sky like i'm high,
begging the ghosts for a reset.
wishing i could drive home,
and you could tell me what would be best—
but i can't, so i'll just pile up some more
regrets,
while i guess at what's next.

to think that you'd forgive me
would hardly be a safe bet,
but i figured i'd at least check.

this ain't a love letter,
but darling, it's the last letter—
until i write you the next letter.

Dear Nora,

this ain't a love letter,
but it's sure gonna sound like one,
cause darling, i'm just not done yet

i'm having one of those days
where i wake up and see your face,
where i wake up in a panicked state,
and i race room to room knowing the truth,
but i'm still searching for you.
so i lay back down, and i pretend again.

i imagine your hand in mine
and i can feel your fingers falling gently
down my weathered cheek.
i notice them withdraw so slightly as they
trace across this mange i've grown in place of
you.

and i feel that excitement as you reach my
cracked lips.
and i shiver as i taste your porcelain skin
again.
and my brow quivers.
and my spine suddenly feels less broken.
and my heart suddenly feels like it's open for
the first time, since the last time.

every part of me can feel you in the air

i lean in.

i can feel the silk of your hair as it
entangles my trembling hand.

i lean in.

i can smell your nerves.

your indecision;
but i lean in.

meanwhile you're wrapped up in him,
and i'm wrapped up in youth.
somehow, i'm both cynical and juvenile—
somehow, i'm both broken and new;
cause i can't move, and i know nothing,
but i know everything i need, and it's not
here with me.

see i miss every part of you;
like all the stories of how you made me
better,
how you held back attacks from inside my own
conscious;
how you kept the demon from prominence.
i miss every part of you;
like all the stories of how you made me into
something presentable—
how you made my dreams seem reasonable—
how something more than this gutter was
suddenly deemed feasible.

i miss every part of you;
like how it all felt so natural—
how it all just fit.

this ain't a love letter,
but when i picture you reading it
i will imagine you still love me.

Dear Nora,

this ain't a love letter,
but this shit's starting to set in,
and i'm tryna figure out why i kill everyone i
let in.

i really thought you were the one—
back when i thought there was one,
you know, someone for someone like me.

i really thought we'd still be fighting
about me feeding the dog too early
when i leave the house at 4 am.
i really thought that i'd be driving to work,
forever smiling about the way your face
crinkles when i sneak back into the bedroom
before walking out the door, just to kiss you
on your brow one last time,
which suddenly really was the last time—
and i'd be all proud about how you'd get so
close to waking up and i'd just freeze:
the only time i ever stood still with you.

nowadays i only sneak back to bed when i
realise i'm not leaving the house this week.
when i'm hiding from commitments i committed
to just so i didn't have to be alone,
because long before the time comes i know i
ain't going,
cause i'm already gone.

this isn't a love letter,
just me hoping you'd share what you did
to feel okay feeling okay so quickly.

Dear Nora,

this ain't a love letter,
it's just what's left over—
words i couldn't say sober.

i ain't said nothing since i saw you,
i just cry and hope it ain't all true,
i just tie this rope up tight—
it's a flawed noose—
i keep this scope aimed at myself,
but i can't shoot.
i'm looking for a hand to finalize my escape
route;
truth be told, i could hold on forever—
i'm stubborn—
but this depression's clever.
it's suggesting dark ideas that i never seem
to fight;
it's suggesting that i sever ties
with anyone who's rooting for my life.
constantly i strategize strategies,
and they all end with a knife...
so maybe it's tonight.

maybe it's tonight.

see darling, i can't change for change's sake—
i stay weighed down by this chain's weight;
who knew broken hearts could still break?
now these lions, they're not tamed,
they're faking—
and all this lying? it's painstaking—
so i lie in wait, and i play patient,

but in my mind i'm pacing, breath racing,
veins tracing every sin i ever put in 'em,
until they make their way across my face—
now my skin's aching,
and all the trauma i've been contemplating?
it surfaces again.

all the trauma surfaces again.

so if i can just get this noose tight,
maybe all this symbolism can shine right;
see, there's a cataclysm behind these eyes,
and all these mannerisms that i despise?
well, they're the other guys.

they're the other guys.

they're the other guys.

i saw your dress—still beautiful—
so give me one last smile,
for all the memories of that other guy,
all those memories that i've defiled.

no more white linen nightmares.
no more nails to dig for in this dirt.
no more black trucks on gravel drives.
no more tear-stained muddy boots.

this ain't a love letter,
it's just me letting grief fester—
cause darling, i ain't never getting better.

Dear Nora,

this ain't a love letter
but sweetness, if i could redo it all—
oh fuck, imagine if i could redo it all.

if i was as smart as i pretend to be,
i'd conjure some kinda machinery
so i could go back
and redo it.

yea, i'd redo it—
i mean let's be straight,
you'd come after a ton of other shit,
but yea, i'd redo it.
of course, while i was back there,
you know there'd be a bit of history
that'd call out to me,
irresistibly.

i'd start at the first time:

interior. kitchen. dawn.

i reach past you,
the air between says it all,
we shoulda kissed,
it woulda bought us another night.

the second time:

exterior. park. dusk.

pretending i wasn't lost,
i was just enjoying the company.

we walked for hours around that lake.
i wonder still,
could it not be both?
could i not be lost, and enjoying the company?

yea, i'd redo it all.
like i already told you.
but i never said i'd change shit,
cause i always loved a story
with an unpredictable twist,
and here i am darling,
all twisted again.

fuck, i'd throw a thousand fits
for a single tryst
that ended with me scared
that i may drown.

but upside down, a smile's a frown
so you know that i enjoyed you,
and i might get a lot wrong,
but i know i'm right
when i say you looked pretty unhappy yourself.

this ain't a love letter,
but i can't help smiling when i get to
thinking
you've sure seen me frown a lot.

Dear Nora,

this ain't a love letter,
cause bargain as i might,
love can't last forever.

i've tried to be part of so many things
that i can't feel a part of this,
a part of that,
a part of anything.
at least i'm a part of my sins,
and yours, i guess.

i'm falling apart at the seams,
cause i'm still dreaming dreams
that we never got a chance to chase,
and i'm still waking to my own panicked
screams,
reaching out for what could be anyone—
reaching out for what could have been—
and punishing those that come running in.

a man should be proud
of where he comes from,
but i ain't.
cause all my pride's gone,
and on top of that,
my pride's gone.
i said we were lions,
but i was wrong,
i guess our pride
was never as strong
as i let on.

and my stride ain't as long

as when i was young—
fuck, i can barely walk at all.
come to think of it,
these hands ain't felt dirt in a while,
ain't been sore from work in a while,
but they hurt, from acting like a child.

seldom do i think of you these days.
instead, i think of how to pay these debts.
and how i'll cover all these solutions
that i've got sitting on lay-away.

and i don't know what's worse,
you not being on my mind
or how i got you off it.

i don't know what hurt i prefer,
but i figure all this suffering is fair,
i mean let's be clear:

i could stop if i wanted to.

this ain't a love letter,
cause who's got time for love
when there's hungry veins to feed?

Dear Nora,

this ain't a love letter,
cause i don't believe anymore,
but i believed yesterday.

i have a hard time finding words in person.
it's easier to write them to no one,
even if your name's atop the page.

i don't think much of you these days,
but it's still enough.
enough to keep pathways to suffering intact.

i might feel lost without,
but i felt just as lost beside you,
no one collects loss like i do.
no one wears flaws, proud, like i do.

i feel in full colour,
not black and white like i used to,
and sure, that was duller,
and sure, i felt smaller,
but i haven't felt safe since.

if saint jude is for lost causes,
then i am fully his.
for i am truly lost in storms of bees
that i can't kill—
or maybe i shouldn't.
i haven't read the news today.

my dreams are big—
like they've always been.
the difference is

lately i don't accomplish 'em.

my dreams are big, like they've always been,
but the content's changed—
my dreams are five fingers of whiskey
flooding down Cocaine covered mountainsides
to drown out what little still remains of
equality.

in said dreams i see you dancing softly
(i think i've seen that dress before),
behind a screen of stretched white linens
soaked in the blood of enemies that never knew
my name,
nor that i exist in wild fantasies of swords
and sorcery.

demons fall apart in sequence:
wings.
fangs.
claws.
regret.

these days, with my body crumbling
like a milk-soaked digestive biscuit,
my teeth sore from all the lies
that i've been forced to chew,
and my hands simply incapable of crafting, or
soothing,
regret is all that's left to hang hope on.

this ain't a love letter,
just a bunch of sad shit
to hang the rope on.

Dear Nora,

this ain't a love letter,
i'm just wondering if you could swing by,
cause i'm still high on last night's high.

i didn't know it was possible to wake up coked
out,
not until you left,
and suddenly i started breaking every record i
ever held,
along with every frame you had me hang
on every wall in a house that's so empty now,
yea, i'm gonna smash everything.
at least records are meant to be broken,
right?

i know you ain't impressed,
but i know that i know a few who would be,
and imma make some calls,
cause i'm sick of snorting paycheques alone,
and i'm sure, with as hard as i work,
i can afford some company.

it's about time that i'm the one being used,
right?
at least maybe i'll feel useful again.

this ain't a love letter,
but if you wanna come grab the rest of your
shit,
maybe do it next weekend, cause i'm on a
fucking rip.

Dear Nora,

this ain't a love letter,
i just gotta talk to someone
before i do something i shouldn't.

i'm sitting here fantasizing about spikes,
picturing perfectly folded squares of white.

i'm thinking of games that require a knife,
i made up a new one, wanna hear it?
it's like russian roulette, but all the
players are chefs
and everybody fucking loses.

i'm a drunk,
we all pretend i'm not,
with some fucking excuse
about this addiction to knots,
but let's not.

let's face truths we never wanted to—
i never loved you, just needed you to prop me
up.
i loved who you made me,
i'm conceited like that,
and i'll agree to these facts,
if you'll concede that it didn't hurt when you
left.

this ain't a love letter,
it's the note i'm leaving
when i say goodbye this evening.

Dear Nora,

this ain't a love letter,
i'm just a little restless,
in the best kinda way.

i'm imaging pinning you up against the wall
again,
i'm on my knees, my mouth doing all it can—
i'm finally speechless—
you drip so thick that i'm deprived of oxygen.
you drip so thick i feel this can't be a sin,
cause i'm being baptized again,
only this time it's consensual.

where are you sleeping?

his arms can't feel like mine.
his hands can't feel like mine,
soft and rough and fine, all at the same time.
they can't leave bruises while healing wounds,
can they?

this ain't a lover letter,
is there such thing as a lust letter?
or did we just make it up?

Dear Nora,

this ain't a love letter,
but i'm thinking about shows again,
hoping i don't run into you.

i hear songs that make my heart hurt,
physically.
i'm not sure it's just this life,
or if someone finally described it right.

the headphones go in and suddenly it's a
fight.
suddenly i'm tryna hold back all this weight
they been piling up on me—
everything you can't see,
everything that's wrong with me.
but i'm a hundred and sixty pounds soaking wet
and i'm swinging blindly at the edge of a
tsunami.

i hear the bridge and i debate jumping,
but the crescendo is barely high enough to
cripple,
and that ain't much of a sendoff.

so here i am, screaming along in a crowd so
loud my voice is drowned out.
thank god, cause i don't want you to hear as i
cry for help.
here i am, begging for an encore i know i
couldn't handle.
here i am, digging all these latest samples
while i'm digging holes again.

this ain't a love letter,
but thanks for all the albums,
i don't know if they're helping.

Dear Nora,

this ain't a love letter,
but i figured we should catch up—
i still like to think you care.

they're passing this assisted death shit,
but i don't meet their checklist.
guess my head ain't ill enough,
or maybe i ain't poor enough.
if that's it, i'm wondering who the fuck is?
you gotta be homeless for them to assist in
you getting the fuck outta here?
nah, probably just gotta be behind on your
taxes.

this shit's deplorable.
so i gone took another leap,
and my hands on the cord,
but i ain't pulling yet.
let's see if this jump means i'm all in,
or i'm still crying cause you ain't calling.

this ain't a love letter,
but i figured i'd reach out,
while they review my application.

Dear Nora,

this ain't a love letter,
just some words i never said,
some words i wish i'd said.

heart attacks and empty hopes,
broken backs and inside jokes,
we weren't us last time we spoke.

the first time that we laid in bed,
more innocent than i can forget
and there's nothing that i regret
more than those last words i never said.

and i break thinking of what i wouldn't do.
and i knew all along what i should do.
but there was nothing that i could do.
my will was frozen over you.

now i'm dreaming about drive-ins
and sleep ins and milkshakes at 2am
and your hand tracing love notes across my
skin.

i'm thinking about my last best friend,
and all the heartbreaks that meant nothing
after you.

we'd talk until the break of dawn—
i still sit up even though you're gone—
having conversations amongst my selves,
every one about my doubts
that you could ever love me now.

those last words i never said...
but i still write to you,
and in those stacks of letters
i'll never send
are those last words i never said,
could you ever love me now?

in the darkest corners of who i am
sits a man that i can't stand
cause he's still crippled over you.

those last words i never said,
could you ever love me now?

cause i could never live you down.
i could never live you down.

those last words i never said,
could you ever love me now?

somedays i wanna come to your door
and beg you to let me in,
but you know better than to talk to strangers.
beneath this coat could be all kinds of sin,
you don't know where this monster's been.

could you ever love me now?

could you ever love me now?

this ain't a love letter,
cause like i said,
could you ever love me now?

Dear Nora,

this ain't a love letter
i just wanna get some shit straight
cause i'm sick of going back and forth.

my heart is mechanical at best,
pumping blood and raising her head
so slightly off my chest.
but there's no metaphorical use in this left.
nothing left to give away,
the pieces barely tangible,
a rebuild hardly manageable.
no one ever sets my mind right like you did—
but she sets my mind in a whole different
direction.
no one ever got me so close to believing in
something
like you did—
but she got me believing in me—
no one ever saw past my memories like you did.
but she don't even know what my memories are
made of,
maybe that's what i need.

and she loves all my scars,
not knowing what they are.

like how under the right light,
they look just like you.

this ain't a love letter,
it's just me picking scabs again,
and you know i know better.

Dear Nora,

this ain't a love letter,
even if i'm using all the right words,
and reading it makes your soul hurt.

suppose i could convince you
to grab what you needed and take off with me—

                    "where would we go?"

anywhere you wanted;

anything you wanted, that's what i'd be then,
cause you were worth everything, anything.
everything i have, everything i had.
anything you want from me, i swear i could do
that.
cause i know i wanna be with you,
and i'm sorry it took this long to figure it
out,
i'm sorry it took that ounce,
it took losing that house.
you, i wanna be with you, no matter what it
does to me,
no matter what you do to me this time,
can't be worse than what i'm doin' now.
no matter who it makes me—
can't be worse than who i am now.
even if you break me—
and darling we both know you'll break me.

but i deserve to be broken.

maybe after you could raise me outta this hole

i live in now,
take me away from who i am now.
take me up, to where we were
when i was so unhappy i needed matches and gas
just to escape you.
when i was so trapped i built ropes from knots
of coke
and climbed sky-high just so i could dive back
down to hell.
break me down, then lift me up to what i
denied me.

maybe you could make me tell what i swore i'd
never tell, degrade myself.
make me what i swore i'd never be: defeated.
make me who i swore i'd never be: the rest of
'em.

this ain't a love letter,
cause i might not love me now,
but i fucking hated me then.

Dear Nora,

this ain't a love letter,
it ain't even for you,
but you're in there somewhere.

my conscience is somewhere north of rome—
without you, i belong alone—
but i'm too afraid for that,
too afraid for simple things,
like nights on a porch staring
at a moon that belonged to you.
too tired for simple things,
like the drive in on a saturday night

i'm a lantern lost in space,
and somehow, it's snowing out here,
but i'm not cold at all.

i'm a lantern lost in space,
and in this whole goddamned abyss of nothing,
i still see your face.
   still hear your voice.
      asking me to come out and play;
but i know you're gone,
and grown men can't play childish games.

i am lost, post your influence;
and in this post-you world
no one wants us,
so we might as well hide in these comics,
might as well drown in narcotics.

i'll go quiet and you'll go lonely,
and everyone that knows me,

that thought i was a riot,
will learn that i'm a whimper.
yea, i'm a liar, i'm a fake—
every part of me on fire is something you
could break—
something i had to make—
so i bury my nose in hate,
knowing i won't survive my immortality
on simply my own fate

this ain't a love letter,
though i did see my first love tonight,
and she still burns my sinuses.

Dear Nora,

this ain't a love letter,
i just need you to fill in the blanks,
cause i can't remember much these days.

you're all but lost.
i can't recall your face.
lost; so you haunt my dreams featureless.
entangled in hair that's probably not quite
the right shade—
unrecognizable.

still, i know it's you.
no one else
has been dream worthy since.

this ain't a love letter,
but i'm finally losing you,
and i ain't never felt fear like this.

Dear Nora,

this ain't a love letter,
i'm just keeping a promise
that i'd always be honest.

i'm on that dope again.
the dog ain't dead,
but i should probably check,
i ain't fed him in a while;
i can't leave this room right now,
and my veins are collapsing,
darling, i'm relapsing again.

tranquility sets in when i mix the powder.
flame to spoon in the afternoon,
i'm about to swoon,
  and miss work again.
    thank god for this white male privilege.

the neighbors know what i'm doing,
and in an hour i'll be half naked
out back staring at the moon.
right after that i'll be staring at pictures
of you,
and me, at the theatre.

funny, that's where i fell in love with her,
the place i always tried to impress you.
and for what it's worth,
i'd still see her,
whereas seeing you, i'd probably see red.
as far as i'm concerned, you're dead.

as far as i'm concerned,

the whole world is Cocaine,
and imma fuckin' get it.
it's here for me to use.
like her,
and her,
and you,

this ain't a love letter,
but someone should know i'm using,
cause shit ain't safe these days.

Dear Nora,

this ain't a love letter,
but there's probably a tree full of books
unwritten
about all the times i've been smitten.

i'm lying awake again,
staring at that unclaimed side of the bed
right next to me.
and my skin's trembling
over secrets that i fear rambling
on nights that i been drinking alone.
on those nights i resemble him,
and all my triumphs are despised.

and every day without you is a crime,
where i steal contempt
from compromised moments of our history.

this ain't a love letter
but i could probably fill a library
with scraps of paper covered in thoughts of
you.

Dear Nora,

this ain't a love letter,
ask anyone,
they'll tell you that i'm over it.

this moon and you, so similar.
they probably saw you coming when they made
it.
they probably sensed your infinite affection
when they named it.
yet i somehow hit the threshold of your
patience;
i guess you got tired of waiting.

and it kinda felt nice being loved for a
while,
but like everything else,
love only lasts so long.
cause like everything else,
it wasn't quite enough 'till it was gone.

see there's this empty pit that's bottomless,
and i could quit this,
but it still demands feedings
—demands a sacrifice—
and the only thing that satisfies
is tears that drop for you.

you could hardly love me sober,
and nowadays i'm all panic,
i'm all looking over my shoulder.
nowadays i'm simultaneously regression and
reinvention,
as i so quickly get older

than anyone ever thought i'd get.

this ain't a love letter,
cause these days i don't believe in that
ask anyone, these days, i'm colder.

Dear Nora,

this ain't a love letter,
unless you wanna get back together,
i could change the mood and address it to you.

i keep thinking of dragging knives across my
skin,
of tracing pretty pictures from my past
and pretending that they're new again.

of all my regrets, the strongest is surviving
you.
i'm barely surviving surviving you.
it's ironic that i crave pain
then complain constantly.
it's funny that i chase suffering
like teenage girls chase boys with shitty
cars.
it's funny that i chase suffering
like boys with shitty cars chase girls with no
pubic hair.

i like my girls to have hair down there.
or not.
it's really not my business.
i like my girls to exist in memories of who i
used to be—
why do you think i'm still writing you?
idealized;
uncomplicated.

this ain't a love letter,
just some words i put together
and figured i'd share with you.

Dear Nora,

this ain't a love letter,
but the dog still knows your name,
so i figured maybe you could visit?

what a fucking path i've started down.
no wonder i'm so cathartic now.
it's an art to act this hard and proud
when all around the mind's a cloud
of memories i can't speak aloud.

all i wanna do is help
save anyone from anything
and then themselves.
save everyone from everything,
but not myself.

immortality be damned,
i know i'm getting old,
cause what used to feel like murder
feels like mercy now.

and i still smell you in her.
and her.
and her.
and anyone else that could use a hand
from these fucking crippled hands of mine.

this ain't a love letter,
but i'm passing through town
if you need the garbage taken out.

Dear Nora,

this ain't a love letter,
and this is probably an over share
but i still think of you when my hands are in
her hair.

i coulda fucked you forever—
lord knows we tried a few times didn't we?
who woulda thought forever could be so finite,
with how infinite it felt when your thighs
squeezed tight against my skull
when i'd bite down and feel your skin break
and i could taste your blood filling cracks
between my teeth

i watched bruises form in the most flattering
places you have to offer
and i've watched you fight the smile i've
earned.
every.
single.
time.
now you're just one of a thousand faces that
wouldn't even recognise mine

this ain't a love letter,
and let's be honest,
it's a couple dozen at most.

Dear Nora,

this ain't a love letter,
well i guess it kinda is
cause i've gone and lost another one.

i'm banging nails again,
and i'm digging trenches—
leather as tight as it's ever been—
it's nothin' fancy, but it's a livin',
and someone's gotta build all these houses no
one can afford.

i've started to water down my gin,
cause i still can't handle the taste,
and nowadays my teeth can't handle the juice i
use to mask it.

darling, what's the use of any of this?
no one will love me weighed down in sin,
not like you used to.

not like you used to.

but suddenly she did.

until she didn't.

now i'm back in my hometown,
but i ain't running around with the old crowd,
but i ain't grown up,
i just aged out.

i wasn't me when i met you,
i was something better.

i wasn't me when i met her either,
i was less than you could fathom,
but i still portrayed that i was better,
ignored the leather,
and told stories of old,
all to get her.

this ain't a love letter,
cause no one seems to want one,
but i'll keep writing anyway.

Dear Nora,

this ain't a love letter,
but i've gone and done some dumb shit,
that we both know i'll get away with.

i'm wrapped up in springsteen songs again,
they're telling me what it means to be a man.
they're telling me to fight this old truck
into reverse
and come back for you.
like you're a possession i forget i knew—
like you're mine to reclaim now that i feel
sane,
but my sanity is gradual,
and at best it's fleeting.

i'm deleting all my memories of functionality
and replacing them with revelries of my time
in captivity.
i'm recreating all my memories of you with
her,
and her,
and her;
but they all smell just like you—
and the bed smells like you—
and the dog gives me that same sideways glance
when i'm not making any sense.
you know the one,
now i'm picturing you giving it to him
and i can already see the blood on my hands,
and i can already taste it
as my fingers brush against my lips
while i smoke this cigarette, post-murder.

the worst part is the pancakes
how do i not burn the pancakes?

this ain't a love letter,
i guess you could call it a confession,
but it's inadmissible, at best.

Dear Nora,

this ain't a love letter,
it's just me facing
the rest of this life alone.

if i am to die without,
let it be tonight.
for i've not changed in all these years
that i've restrained from seeing you—
i could find you if i wanted to.

what you'd think of what i've become
tops each and every one of my fears:
the darkness.
the noise.
the repeated memories that forever taint my
dreams.

the disappointment in your eyes
and the pity in your words;
i can taste them in every stalk of hay.
in every hint of gasoline that rushes to my
heart.

this ain't a love letter,
it's just me stalling
the inevitable thoughts of dying alone.

Dear Nora,

this ain't a love letter,
just me stewing in my grief
and hoping you'll grieve too.

i spent the day looking at old wounds.
funny,
i remember a different man earning
each and every one of these scars.

funny,
when all the wine is drained,
and all the whiskey has been filtered through
gravel,
i know not of the cause of these marks,
but i remember the man i was when i first wore
'em.

it's funny,
cause when i close my eyes
it's like just yesterday i was sitting on a
metal bridge
in the middle of some tiny forest that felt
huge at the time,
with curls running past my shoulders.

and memories weren't memories yet.
just moments.

this ain't a love letter
i'm just reminiscing
on every fault that's mine.

Dear Nora,

this ain't a love letter,
it's an introduction
to someone you ain't met yet.

cause me,
i'm already gone,
i walked out with you.
what's left in my place
might look just like me,
might sound just like me,
might even be dressed up as me,
but it ain't.

it's something different, something sinister.
something designed to survive through the
darkest dark.

what grows around whatever was left after,
it knows my voice.
it knows all my fears,
my secrets too.
it knows exactly how to use it all to
grow stronger every fucking day.
and it still looks just like me,
no matter the size of the storm that surrounds
it.

but it's not me, i'm already gone,
i walked out with you.

this ain't a love letter,
bit early for love yet,
we only just met.

Dear Nora,

this ain't a love letter
it's a list of shit
i gave up for you.

probably shouldn't have bought those concert
tickets way back when i did.
any contact with a friend's ex is a bad idea
for a guy like me.

i guess i'll start there,
cause he sure as fuck ain't answering
if i call, right?

what else…
     what else?

chasing girls
that never made me question
what i was doing with myself.
i definitely miss that.
these days i can't lay with anyone
that doesn't have something to say about
everything.

the delusion of being content with a generic
middle-class life.
of smiling when i walk into a bar on a friday
night,
suddenly surrounded by people i've known my
whole fucking life.
let's all talk about our work week, that'll be
fun…

Cocaine. not permanently, obviously.
otherwise i wouldn't have to talk to you in
letters that probably aren't even going to the
right address these days.

of course, i didn't know i was about to give
up ever being happy again.
but i was.
and i did.

at least you showed me what i could be,
now i get to lay here, strung out,
grasping for someone i'll never be again.

this ain't a love letter.
i'm just grasping,
for someone i'll never see again.

Dear Nora,

this ain't a love letter,
but i've been thinking of our first memory,
and i finally found something to compare it
to.

i don't remember my first kiss.
or when i realised that words in my head
were a lot friendlier on paper.

but i remember the first time i did Cocaine,
and i remember when i realized what you meant
to me,
and i remember when i realized that i realized
too late.

it's fitting really,
of all the people i've been with,
in all the mes,
i've managed to sell the world,
it seems only right i think of you
in the same breath as that first high;
even if you represent the best in me,
and the worst.

these two moments,
two decisions made...

fuck it i'm going in.

they defined my entire life—
at least life thus far,
i ain't as old as i sound,
or as old as i like to pretend.

you're a part of all that's good in me,
a part of all that works.
that's all gone now,
i may never work again.

this ain't a love letter,
but i sure do think fondly
of you and Cocaine.